Amazing
ORIGAMI BOXES

Tomoko Fuse
the great Japanese origami master

Amazing
ORIGAMI BOXES

Dover Publications, Inc.
Mineola, New York

Bibliographical Note

Amazing Origami Boxes, first published by Dover Publications, Inc., in 2018, is an unabridged English translation of the work originally published by NuiNui, Switzerland, in 2017.

Library of Congress Cataloging-in-Publication Data

Names: Fuse, Tomoko, 1951- author.
Title: Amazing origami boxes / Tomoko Fuse.
Other titles: Boâites en origami d'exception. English
Description: Mineola, New York : Dover Publications, 2018. | "Amazing Origami
  Boxes, first published by Dover Publications, Inc., in 2018, is an unabridged English
  translation of the work originally published by NUINUI, Switzerland, in 2017."
Identifiers: LCCN 2017051029| ISBN 9780486822464 (paperback) | ISBN 048682246X
Subjects: LCSH: Origami. | Box making. | BISAC: CRAFTS & HOBBIES / Origami. |
  CRAFTS & HOBBIES / Papercrafts.
Classification: LCC TT872.5 .F8713 2018 | DDC 736/.982—dc23
LC record available at https://lccn.loc.gov/2017051029

Printed in China by RR Donnelley
82246X01   2018
www.doverpublications.com

Texts and diagrams
Tomoko Fuse

Photographs
Dario Canova

INTRODUCTION

. . . .

Selecting the most appropriate paper, thinking about where and how we will use our box, and imagining the places and people with which it will come into contact with is great fun. And by varying the type of paper and color combinations we can create a range of different effects.

Despite being a very simple object, an origami box contains the emotions of the person who created it. With this in mind, I warmly offer you this book and hope that it will inspire a sort of secret smile between the person who builds the box and the person who uses it.

In origami there is no doubt that the primary pleasure comes from folding the paper. But there is another pleasure, which comes immediately afterwards, and that lies in being able to admire and use the objects created. From this point of view, making origami boxes can provide a great sense of satisfaction.

This book contains a wide variety of box models, some very easy, others more complex, all of which can be made with a single sheet of paper. In most cases, the essential structure of the box, made from a single sheet, is accompanied by additional elements, such as a reinforced base or a divider, which can be made using further sheets. This also gives you the opportunity to enjoy creating various color combinations.

SUMMARY

· ·

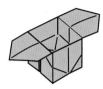

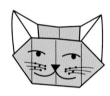
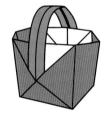

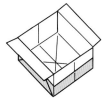
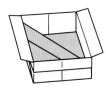
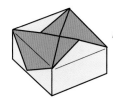

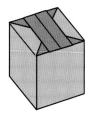

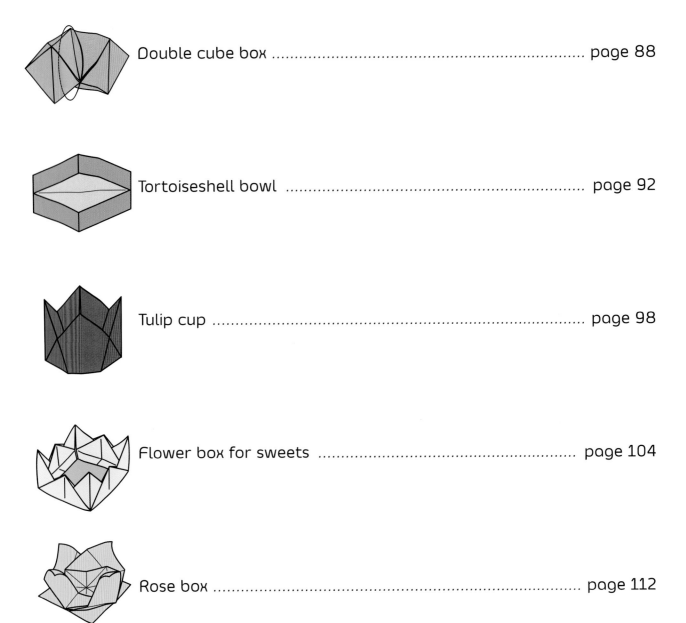

BIOGRAPHY

• • • • • • • • • • • • • • • • •

Tomoko Fuse first came across origami when she was seven years old; she began making paper models during a stay in hospital. In around 1980, well ahead of her time, she became so passionately dedicated to making origami models, using several sheets folded separately, that she earned the nickname "the queen of modular origami".

Constantly experimenting with new ways of folding paper, she began to focus on making geometric shapes and even designed industrial products such as lampshades and the collection of Origami Pots.

1951 She is born in the province of Niigata. She graduates in Garden Design from the University of Chiba.

1986 She moves to Yamamura Yasaka, in the province of Nagano, and begins practising origami professionally.

1987 She is invited to Italy by CDO (Centro Diffusione Origami).

1989 On behalf of the Japan Foundation, she visits the UK, Germany, Holland, Poland and Bulgaria.

1990 She is invited by Origami USA (the American National Association for origami).

1991 She is invited by various organisations and associations to Paris, Germany and Spain.

1994 She organizes the second OSME (an international scientific origami convention) that takes place in Otsu, making a valuable contribution to the success of the event.

1998, 2000, 2003 She is invited to the Festival of Origami in Charlotte, USA.

1998 She is one of three Japanese origami artists invited to exhibit at the Paris origami exhibition held at the Louvre.

1999 She is invited by the Canada Origami Group and the Japanese-German Association.

2002 She is invited to exhibit at the *On Paper* exhibition, held in the UK with sponsorship by the Crafts Council. At the third OSME, which takes place in America, she presents Origami Pots, the result of research conducted with three other colleagues. In the same year, Origami Pots receives a patent.

2003 She is invited to exhibit at the *Origami* exhibition, held at the American Folk Art Museum.

2004 In April, she holds a solo exhibition in Israel, at the Hankin Gallery. In September, she holds another solo exhibition in Germany, at the Bauhaus, and is invited by the British Origami Society.

2005 One of her works is chosen for the poster of the *Masters of Origami* exhibition in Salzburg.

2006 She is invited by the Indian Origami Association.

2008 She is a guest at the general conference held on the occasion of the 25th anniversary of the Dutch Origami Association.

2009 She holds the *Yorokobi* (Happiness) exhibition in Germany, alongside her husband, an artist working with wood.

2010 In March, she is invited by the origami associations of Colombia and Brazil. In August, she is invited by the Ohio CenterFold. In September, she exhibits her origami at the Tokyo Yurakucho Forum. In October, in Germany, to celebrate the centenary of the Fröbel Museum, she once again holds the *Yorokobi* exhibition alongside her husband.

2011 The *Yorokobi* exhibition is transferred to Hittisau, in Austria.

2012 She is one of the artists invited to the traveling American *Folding Paper* exhibition.

2013 In May, she is invited by a group of origami artists in Germany and France. In November she is invited by Mexico Origami.

2014 In July, she is invited by the Ohio CenterFold. In September, on behalf of the Japan Foundation, she visits India and Bhutan. In November, she makes large inlaid models for the Axia South Cikarang Hotel, in Indonesia.

2015 Alongside Heinz Strobl she participates in the *Space Folding* exhibition in Schahof, Germany. In December, she is invited to Italy by the CDO (Centro Diffusione Origami).

2016 In April, she holds a solo exhibition at the Museum of Modern Art Toyoshina in Azumino.

Bibliography

Tomoko Fuse has a hundred books to her name, including *Unit Polyhedron Origami*, *Origami Four Seasons*, *Modular Origami* and *Amazing Origami - Introduction*. Some of these have also been translated into English, German, Italian and Korean. She has also published several essays on life in the mountain village of Yamamura: *Hard-working Mountain Life* and the illustrated volume *Look. What I've Found! Delicacies from the Plains and Mountains*. *Spiral*, a collection of helix, shell and vortex models, was published in 2012.

ftomoko@yasakanet.ne.jp

SYMBOLS KEY

Degree of difficulty

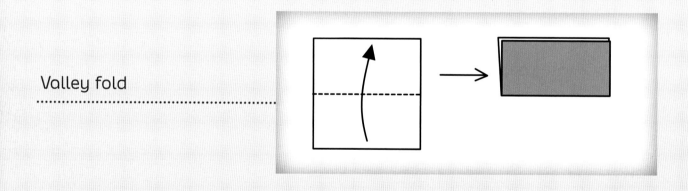

●○○	Medium
●●○	Medium to advanced
●●●	Advanced

Valley fold

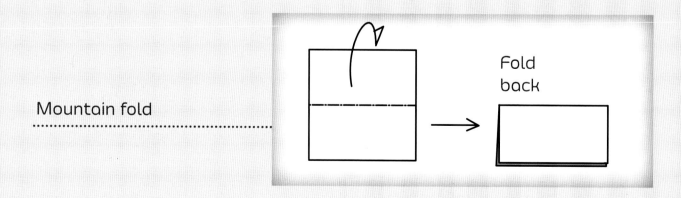

Mountain fold

Fold back

Fold and unfold

Fold into equal parts

Fold so that the
○ symbols meet

Fold so that the
● symbols meet

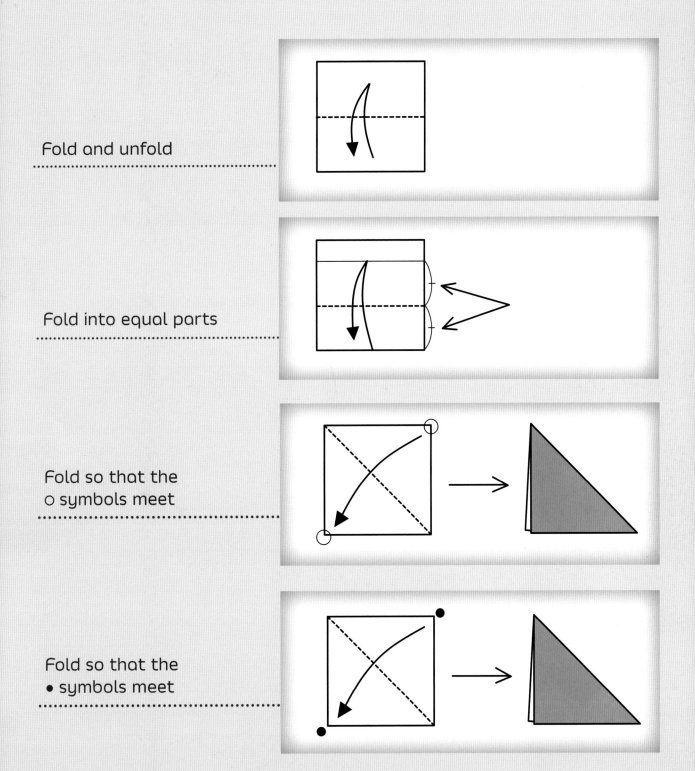

Make a crimp
or accordion fold

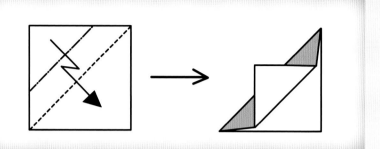

Insert

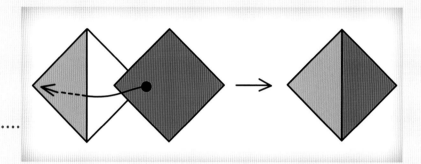

Turn over
the paper

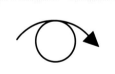

Enlargement

Reduction
in scale

Rotate
the paper

Result after
several modules
have been joined
together

The fold only involves
the upper layer, allow
the lower layer to come
out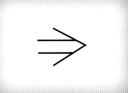

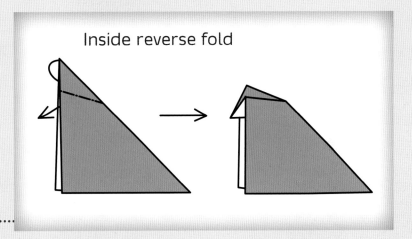

Reverse folds

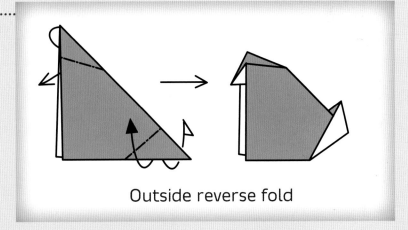

The models shown in this book will be sufficiently solid without the need for glue. However, if you need to strengthen a model, do not hesitate to glue it.

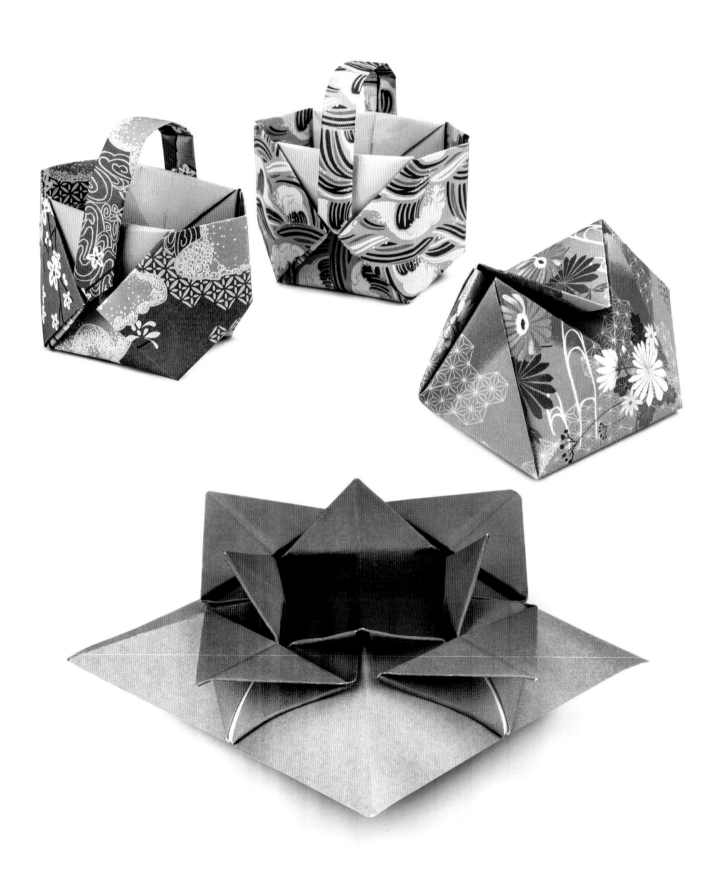

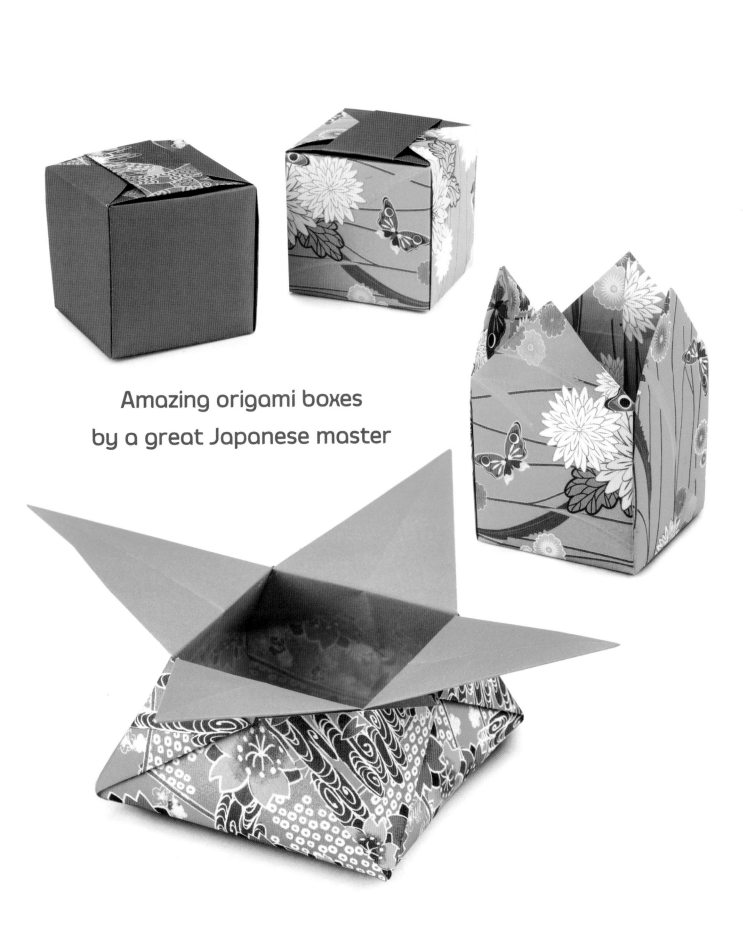

Amazing origami boxes
by a great Japanese master

Paper:
standard
15 x 15 cm
(6 inches x 6 inches)
or 20 x 20 cm
(8 inches x 8 inches)

Interlocking box
(made from squares)

Make the two modules and insert
one inside the other.

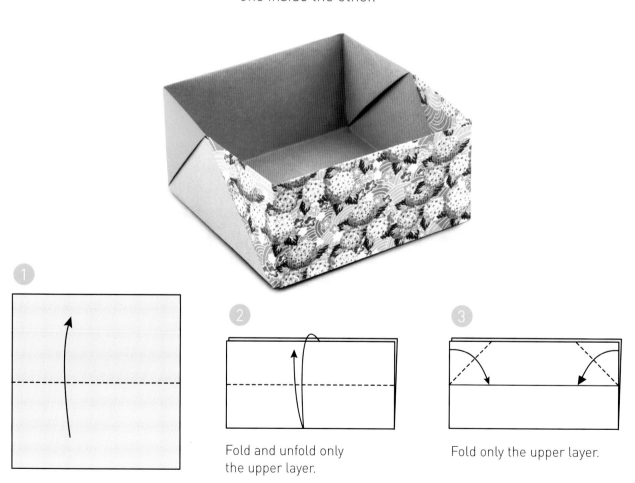

1

2

Fold and unfold only
the upper layer.

3

Fold only the upper layer.

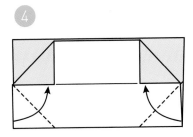

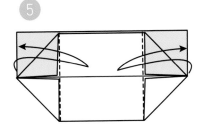

Mark the folds clearly.

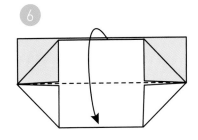

Fold only the upper layer.

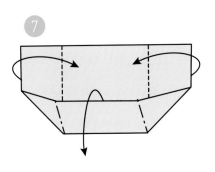

Lift the edges.

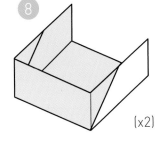

(x2)

The module.

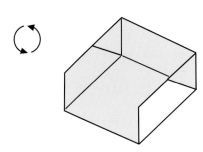

JOINING THE MODULES TOGETHER.

Insert one module inside the other by reversing the interlocking order.

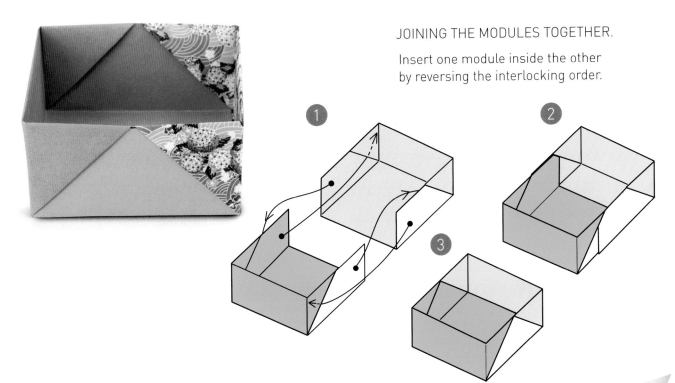

Paper:
standard
15 x 15 cm
(6 inches x 6 inches)

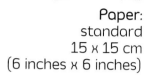

Party dish 1

Once the outer casing has been made, a second layer can be inserted.
This helps the model become more solid.

OUTER CASING

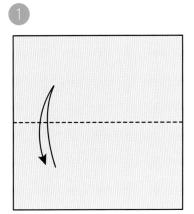

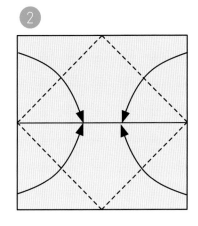

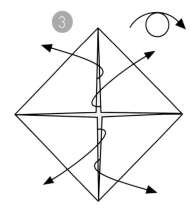

Open and turn over the paper.

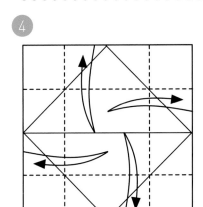

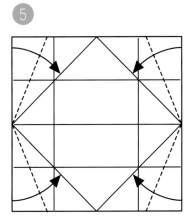

Mark the folds.

Bring the upper and lower parts into the middle, then fold all the flaps and flatten them.

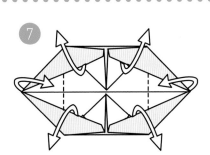

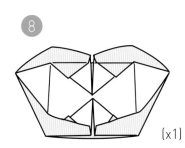

Lift the edges to provide depth.

(x1)

INSIDE LAYER

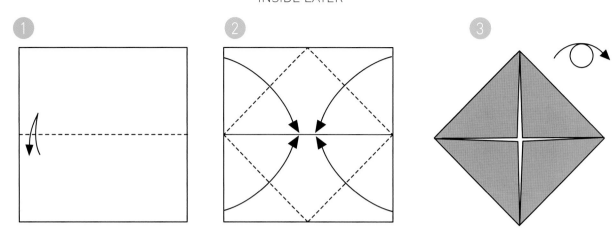

Insert this second layer inside the outer casing.

JOINING THE MODULES TOGETHER

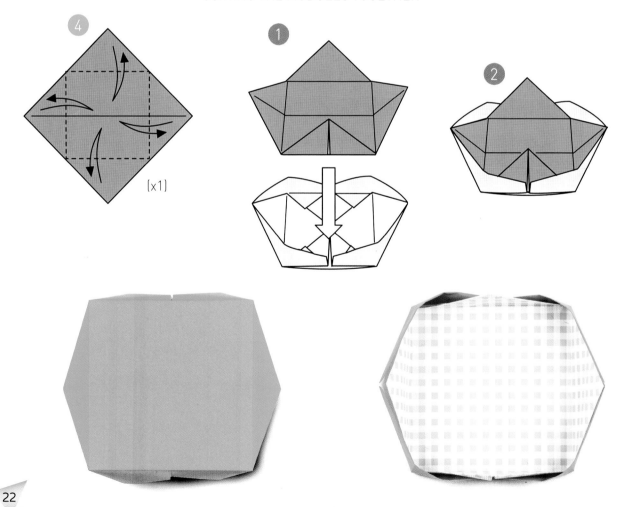

(x1)

Paper:
standard
15 x 15 cm
(6 inches x 6 inches)

Party dish 2

This is a dish with decorative frill. Also in this case, inserting a second layer inside the outer casing makes the model more solid.

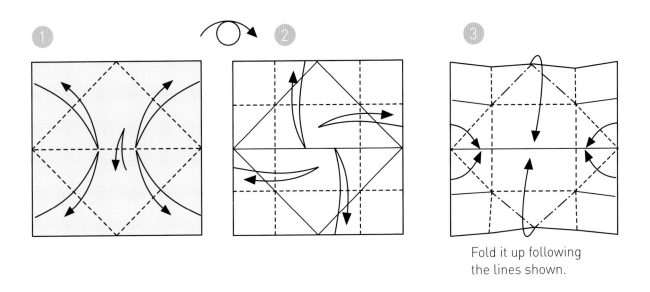

Fold it up following the lines shown.

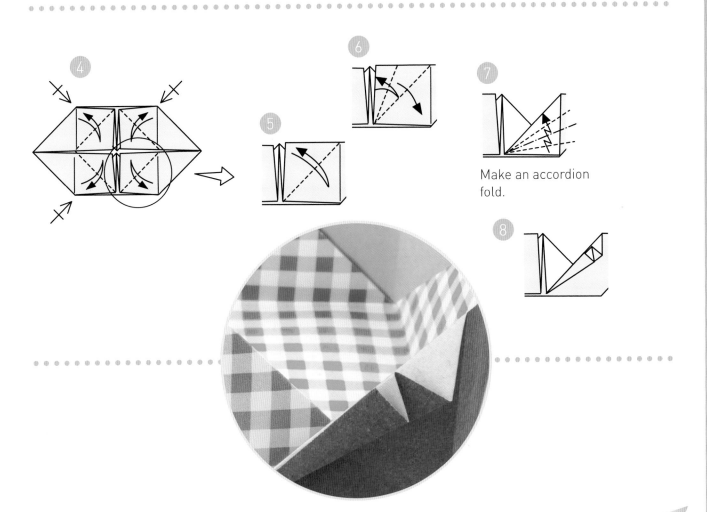

Make an accordion fold.

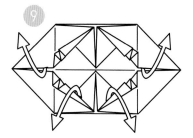

Lift the edges to provide depth.

JOINING THE MODULES TOGETHER

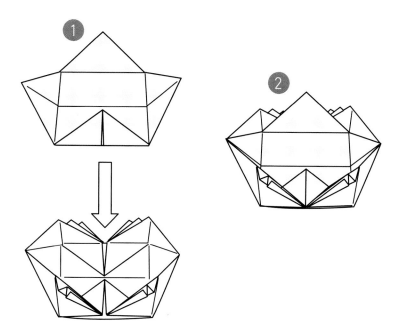

Insert the inner layer into the outer casing.

Paper:
standard
15 x 15 cm
(6 inches x 6 inches)

Bird box

This box looks like a bird.

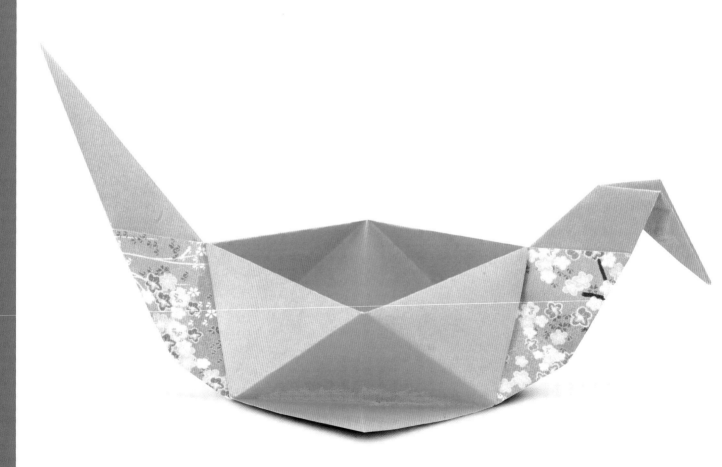

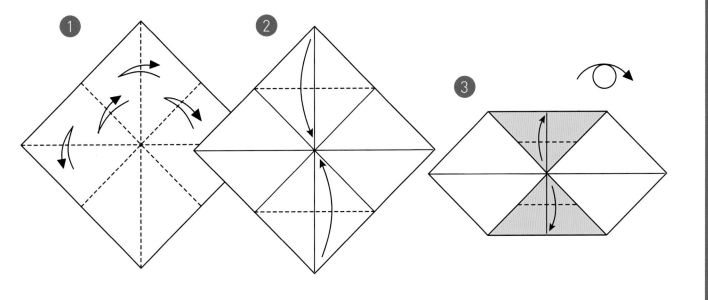

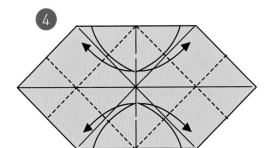

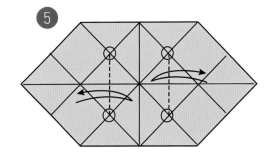

Mark the folds up to
the O symbols.

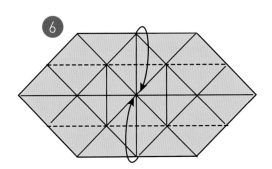

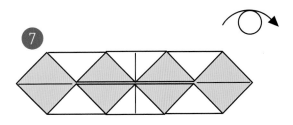

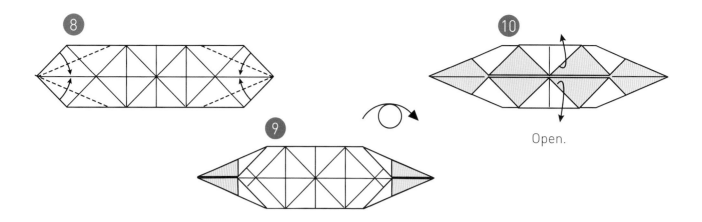

8

9

10

Open.

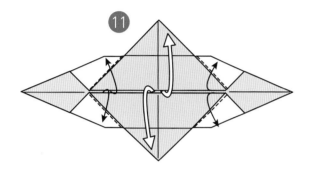

11

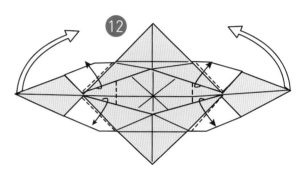

12

Open the inside by lifting the two edges.

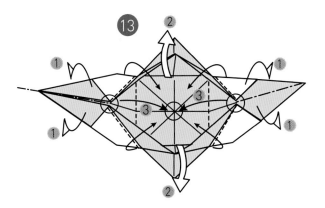

13

1) Fold the two triangles on the left and right in half.
2) Open the lower and upper flaps.
3) Bring the O symbols together.
Finally, use two fingers to hold the triangles at the point (1) and lift.

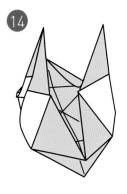

14

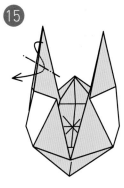

15

Make an inside reverse fold.

16

Adjust the completed bird.

17

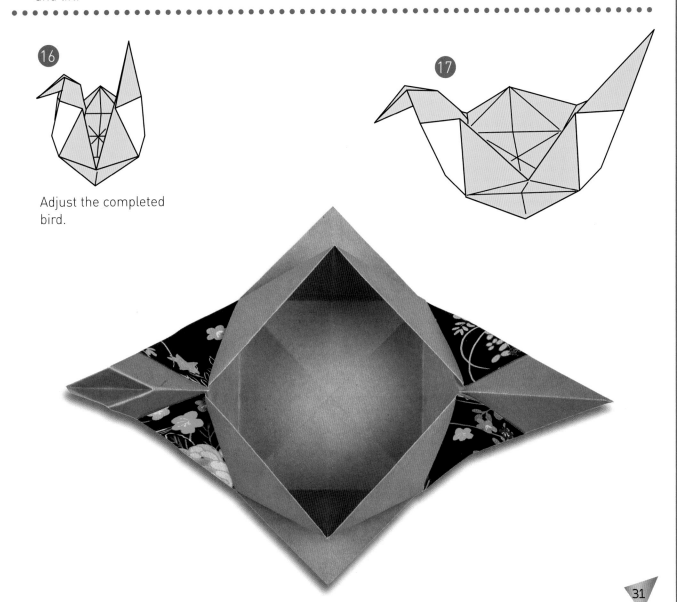

Paper:
standard
15 x 15 cm
(6 inches x 6 inches)

Incense holder with pointed triangles
(made from squares)

This is a type of traditional box with four protruding triangular spikes.
Up to diagram 7, the steps are the same as the "square base," but you could
also use the model 12 template, used for the box (traditional Japanese origami),
following diagrams 1 to 4 on page 67.

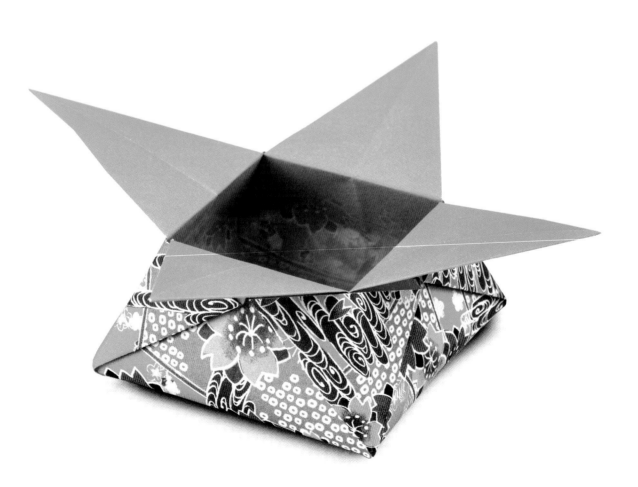

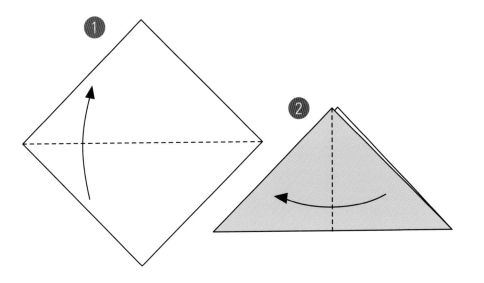

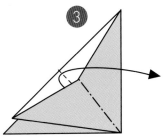

By pushing a finger into
the pocket, open it up and
flatten it.

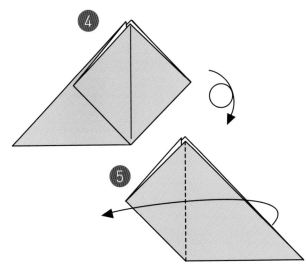

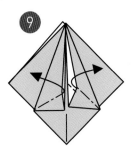

Fold only the upper layer
of the triangle, bringing it
down towards the opposite
edge.

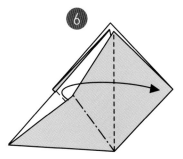

By pushing a finger into
the pocket, open it up
and flatten it.

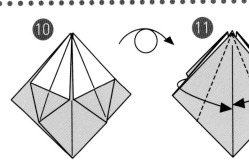

Square base.

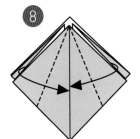

By pushing a finger into
the pocket, open it up
and flatten it.

 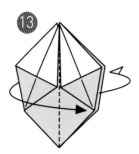 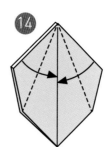 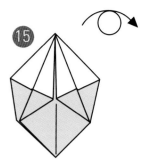

Make a book fold.

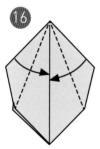 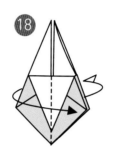 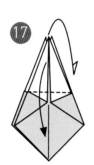 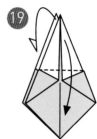 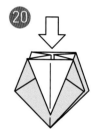

Make a book fold.

Open up the inside by pulling out the four ends. The base is shaped by pressing upwards and inwards.

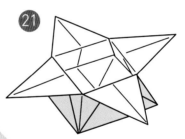

Paper:
standard
15 x 15 cm
(6 inches x 6 inches)

Offering box
(traditional Japanese origami)

The *sanbo* is a ritual box in which food offerings are placed.
When made using origami it can become a useful container.

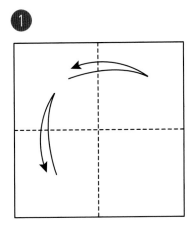

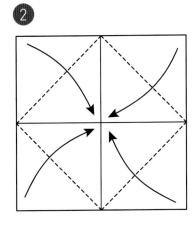

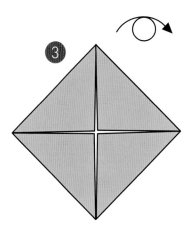

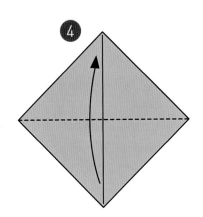

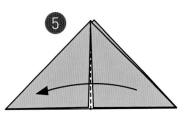

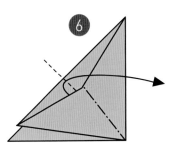

By pushing a finger
into the pocket, open
it up and flatten it.

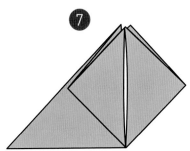

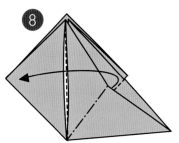

By pushing a finger
into the pocket, open
it up and flatten it.

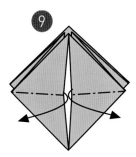

By pushing a finger
into the pocket, open
it up on both sides.

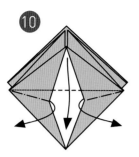

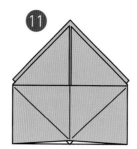

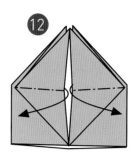

While opening both sides
fold down the top point.

Turn over the paper and
repeat the steps in diagrams
9 and 10.

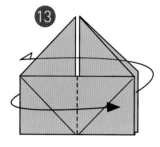

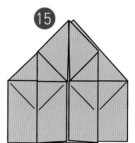

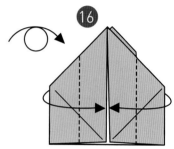

Make a book fold.

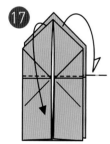

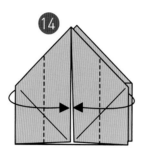

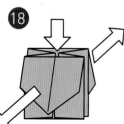

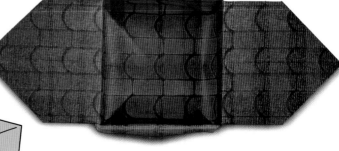

Open up the inside by lifting
the handles up to a horizontal
position then shape the
completed box.

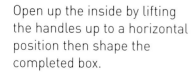

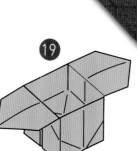

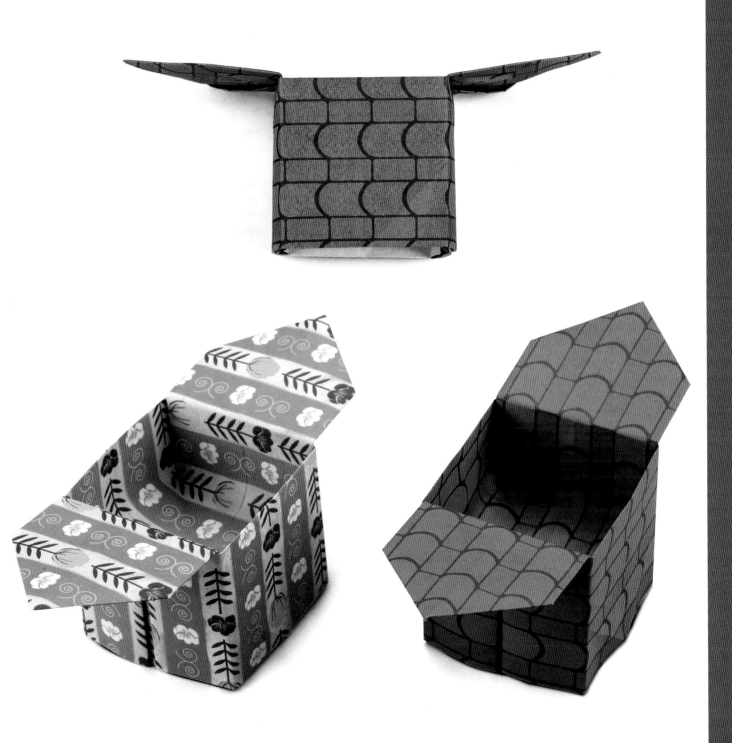

Paper:
standard
15 x 15 cm
(6 inches x 6 inches)

Paintbrush rinsing pot
(traditional Japanese shape)

When you have finished folding, a pretty, round bowl will appear.

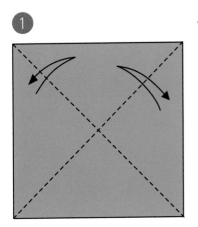

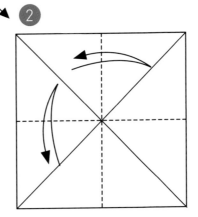

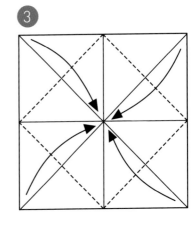

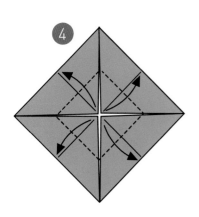

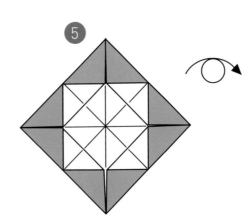

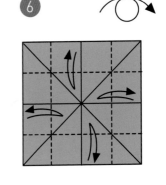

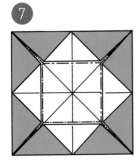

Squeezing the four corners between two fingers will allow the central square to take on a shape reminiscent of a table.

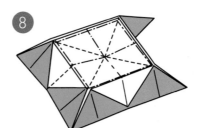

Press in the center and push down.

Shape the paper to create two layers on both sides and flatten.

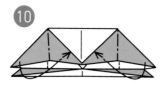

10

Turn the four corners back inside.

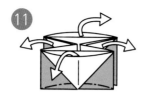

11

Open it up on all sides then shape the finished pot.

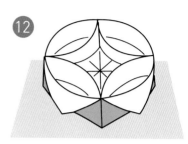

12

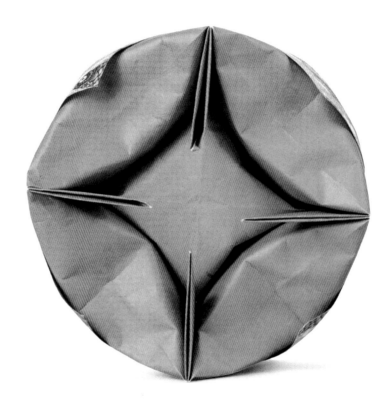

Paper:
standard
15 x 15 cm
(6 inches x 6 inches)

Cat-head box
with triangular handles

This pretty box can also be decorated.

1

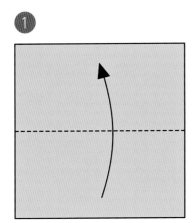

2

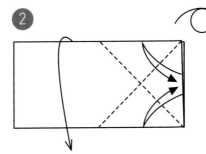

Mark the folds on both layers together, then unfold.

3

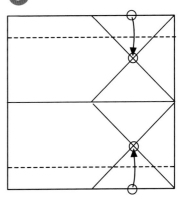

Fold so that the O symbols meet.

4

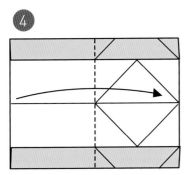

Fold in half.

5

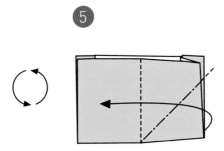

6

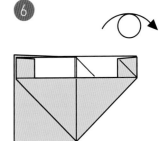

7

8

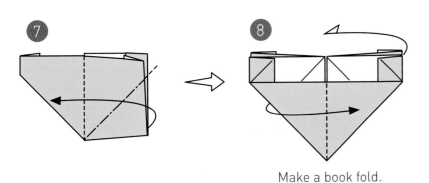

Make a book fold.

9

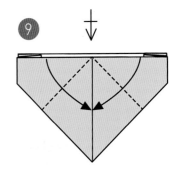

Fold the rear part in the same way.

10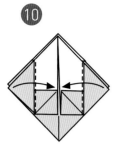

Repeat the same step on the back.

11

Insert the triangles into the pockets and repeat on the back.

12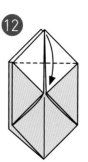

13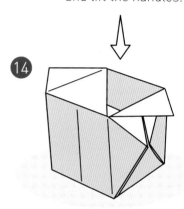

Open the inside, flatten the base and lift the handles.

12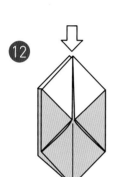

Open the inside and flatten the base.

14

BOX WITH TRIANGULAR HANDLES

13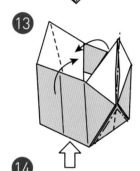

Press the base so that it goes back inside the model.

14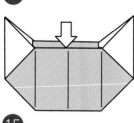

Open up the inside again and shape the finished box.

15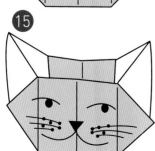

You may want to draw a cat's face on your box.

CAT-HEAD BOX

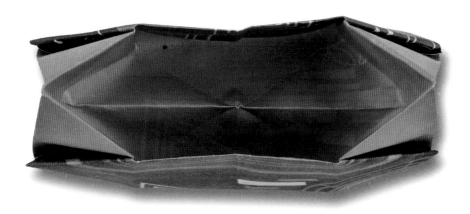

Paper:
standard
20 x 20 cm
(8 inches x 8 inches)

Basket with triangular handles

Make a basket by giving the box with triangular handles a strap.
The bigger the sheet of paper you use the easier it will be to make.

A sheet of paper the same size as that used for the box with triangular handles.

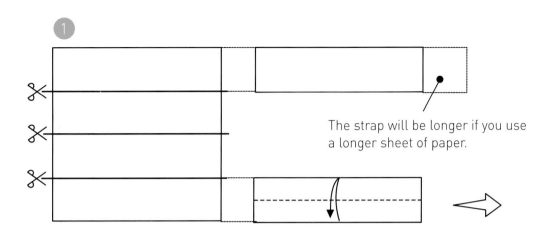

The strap will be longer if you use a longer sheet of paper.

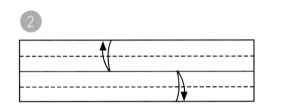

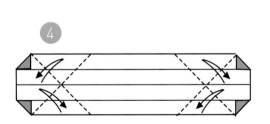

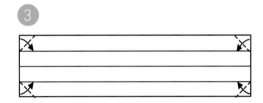

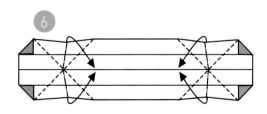

Close it by bringing the lines shown together.

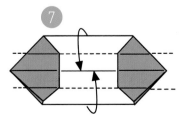

Fold both the edges towards the center.

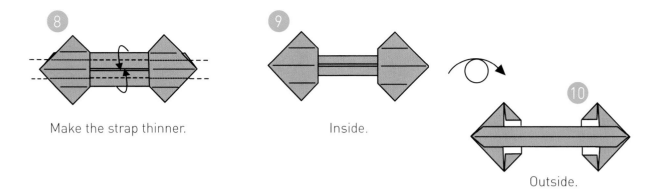

Make the strap thinner.

Inside.

Outside.

JOINING THE MODULES TOGETHER
Insert into the openings of the box with triangular handles by bringing the O symbols together.

Box with triangular handles.

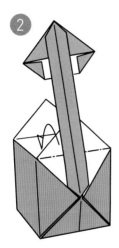

After inserting the strap, close it by folding the triangular handles inside.

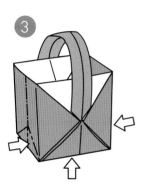

Shape the basket.

Paper:
standard
20 x 20 cm
(8 inches x 8 inches)

Flower box
(A and B)

This is a pretty flower-shaped container that can be made to suit your taste.
As you will see, for example, the base of both boxes is not flat but slightly rounded.

Flower box A

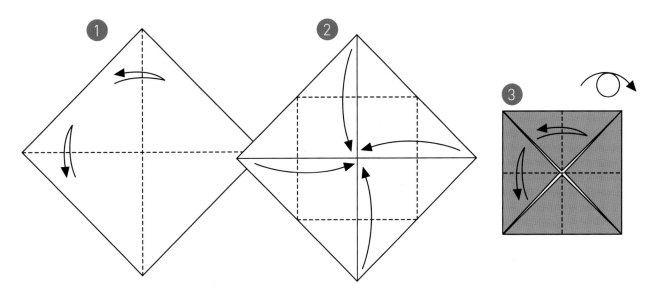

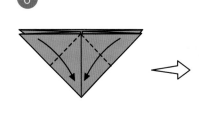

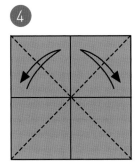

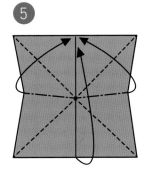

Fold it up following
the lines shown.

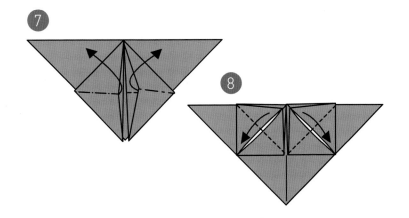

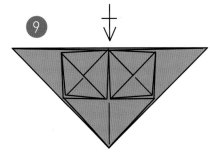

Repeat the steps carried
out in diagrams 7 and 8
on the back.

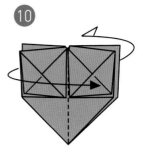

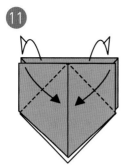

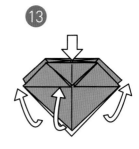

Make a book fold.

Open at the point shown by
the upper arrow and flatten
the base, then lift the petals
and shape the box.

The base of the box
is not actually flat but
slightly rounded.

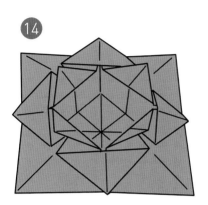

FLOWER BOX A

Flower box B

From diagram 8 of flower box A.

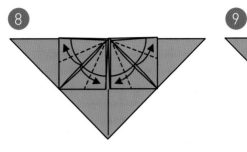

8

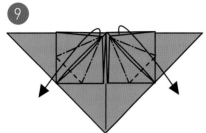

9

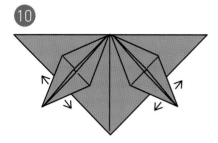

10

Pull out the layer underneath.

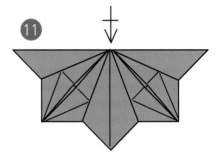

11

Repeat the steps carried out in diagrams 8, 9 and 10 on the back.

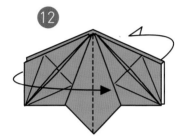

12

Make a book fold.

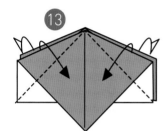

13

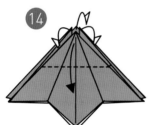

14

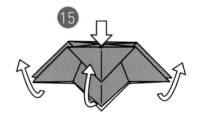

15

Open at the point shown by the upper arrow and flatten the base, then lift the petals and shape the box.

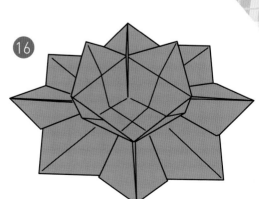

16

FLOWER BOX B

Paper:
standard
15 x 15 cm
(6 inches x 6 inches)

Flower bowl

Make the folds shown step-by-step and you will see
a flower-shaped bowl appear.

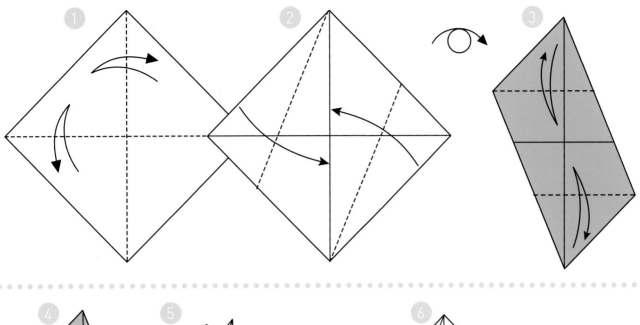

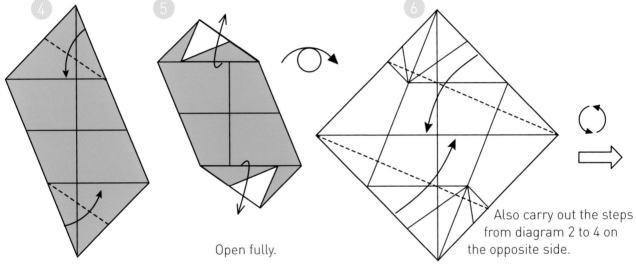

Open fully.

Also carry out the steps from diagram 2 to 4 on the opposite side.

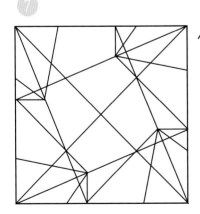

The sheet with all the folds marked.

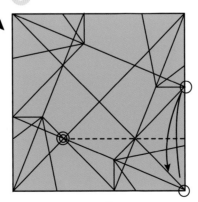

Fold to symbol ◎, bringing the O symbols together.

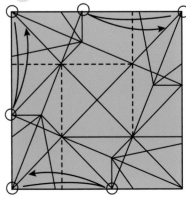

Carry out the same step three more times.

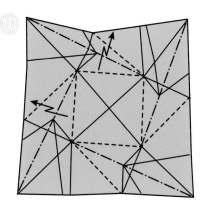

Make a crimp by bringing the
lines shown together to give
more depth.

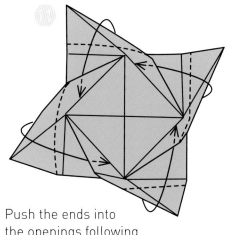

Push the ends into
the openings following
the marked folds.

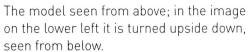

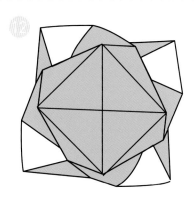

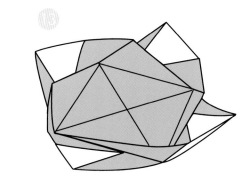

The model seen from above; in the image
on the lower left it is turned upside down,
seen from below.

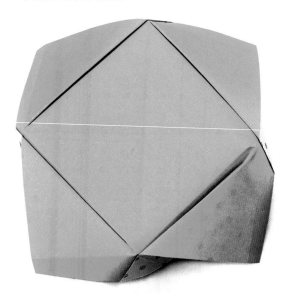

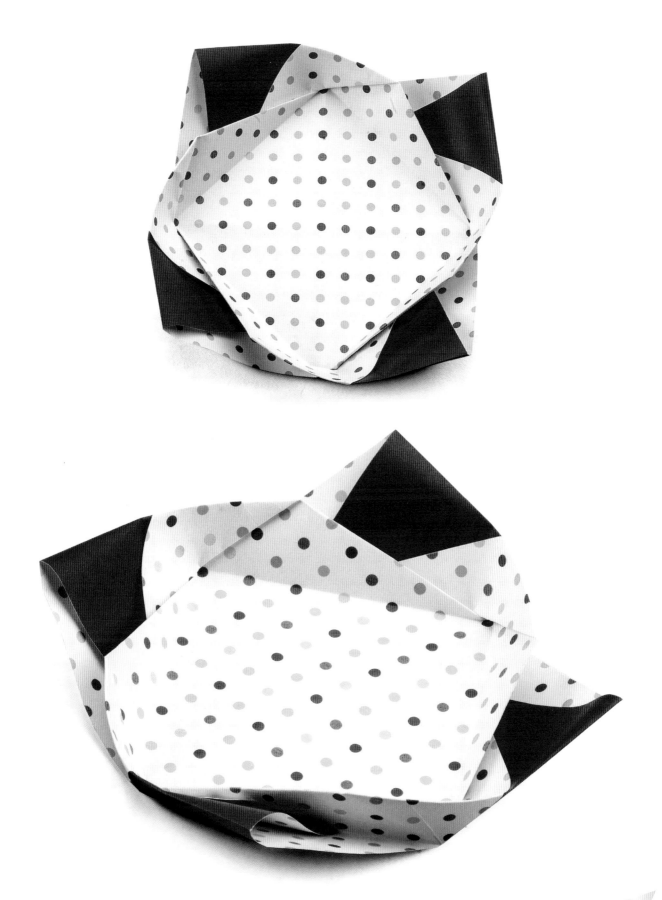

Paper:
standard
15 x 15 cm
(6 inches x 6 inches)

Box
(traditional Japanese origami)

The so-called "square base," achieved with the first four diagrams,
can also be made using the steps from diagrams 1 to 6 for the incense holder
with pointed triangles. Choose the method you prefer.

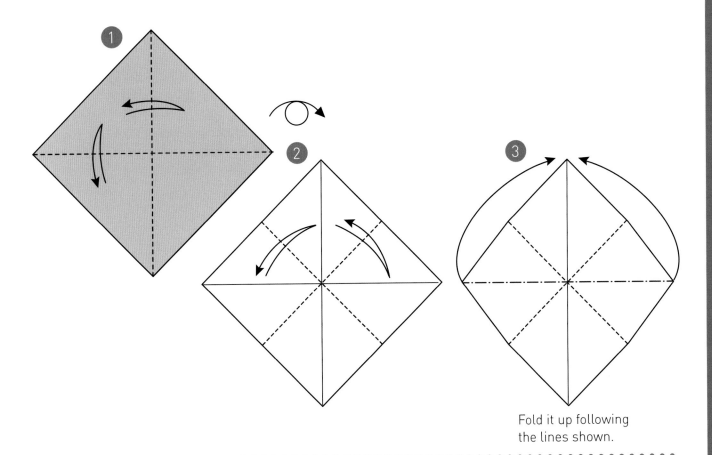

Fold it up following
the lines shown.

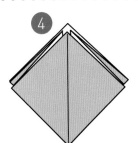

SQUARE BASE

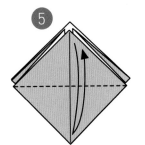

In diagrams 5, 6, 7, and
8 make the folds on the
upper layer only.

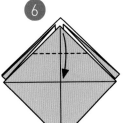

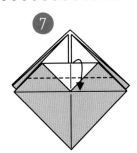

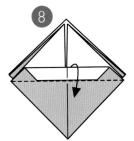

Carry out the same
steps on the back.

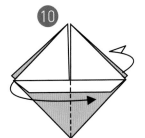

Make a book
fold.

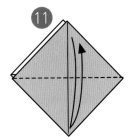

Make the folds
on the upper
layer only.

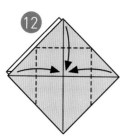

Make the folds on
the upper layer only.

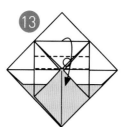

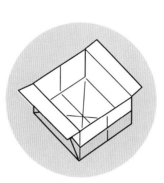

Repeat the steps carried out
in diagrams 11, 12 and 13 on
the back.

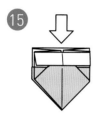

Open the inside, flatten the
base and lift the handles.

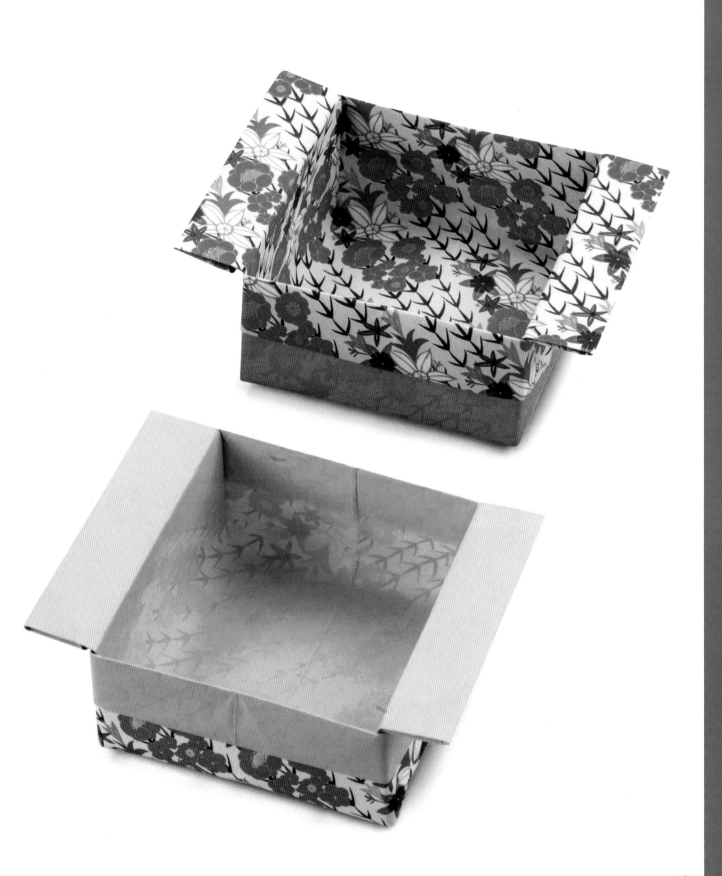

Paper:
standard
15 x 15 cm
(6 inches x 6 inches)

Diagonal box divider

Boxes can be strengthened using a diagonal divider.
This fits perfectly. It can also be used for the *masu* box that follows.
If you find the divider difficult to insert use a slightly
smaller sheet of paper, as in B.

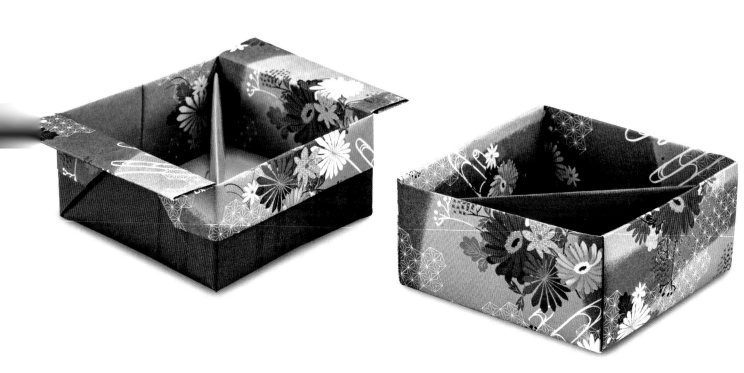

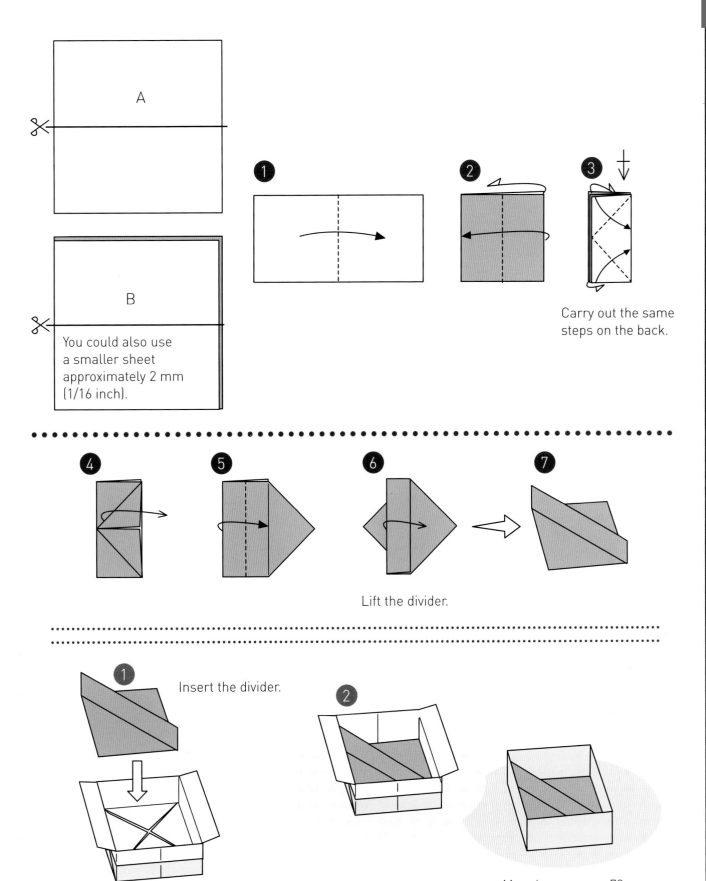

A

B

You could also use
a smaller sheet
approximately 2 mm
(1/16 inch).

Carry out the same
steps on the back.

Lift the divider.

Insert the divider.

Masu box on page 72
with divider.

Paper:
standard
15 x 15 cm
(6 inches x 6 inches)

Masu box

With a little extra work you can give your *masu* a lid and a base, making the box even more complete. It is worth taking the time because the lid and the base are made using an almost identical process.

BASIC *MASU*: MAIN MODEL

The traditional Japanese *masu* can be made in different versions. We will start with the basic model.

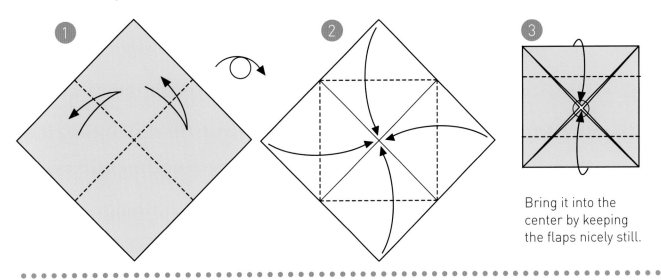

3

Bring it into the center by keeping the flaps nicely still.

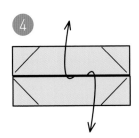

4

Lift it by opening the inside flaps together.

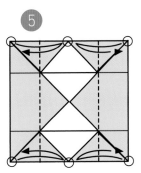

5

Mark the folds then open the upper and lower flaps.

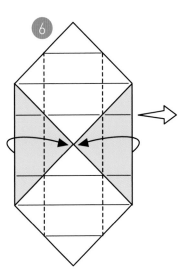

6

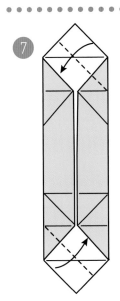

7

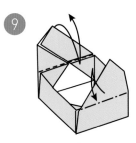

8

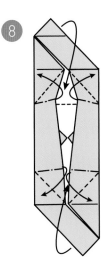

9

Mark the folds clearly.

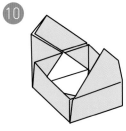

10

Temporarily open up the model at diagram 10 to get diagram 11.

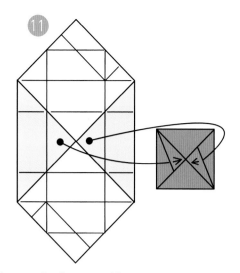

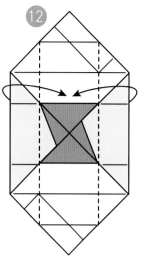

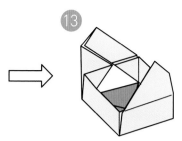

Insert the base and insert
the ends of the box inside it.

Repeat the steps carried out
in diagrams 8 and 9.

Once the base is inserted,
fold the model again by
returning to diagram 10.

WEDGE BASE

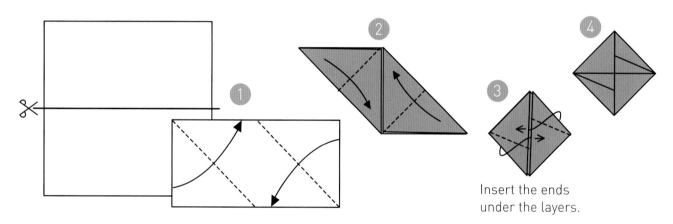

Insert the ends
under the layers.

LID

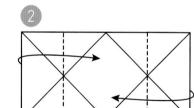

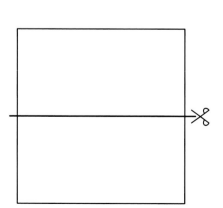

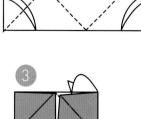

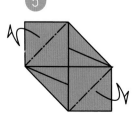

Inside reverse fold.

Mark the folds.

JOINING THE MODULES TOGETHER

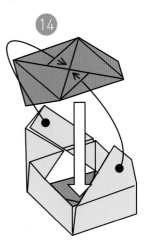

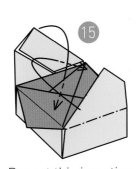

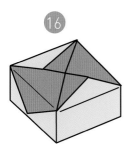

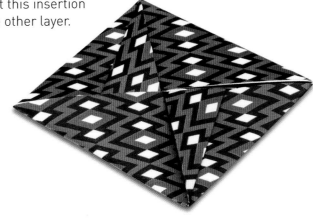

Insert into the openings.

Repeat this insertion for the other layer.

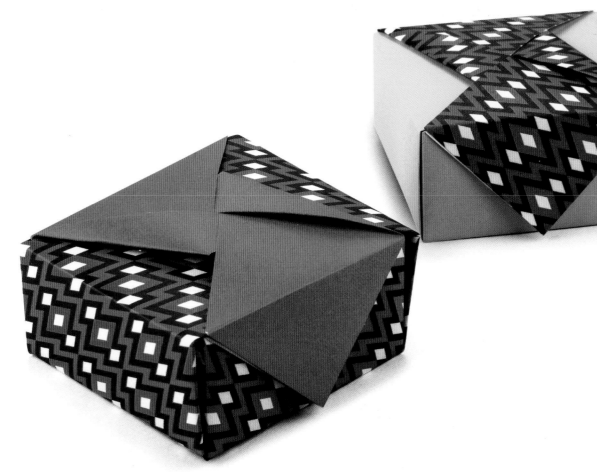

Paper:
standard
15 x 15 cm
(6 inches x 6 inches)

Square bowl

This square bowl will look even better if you use a wedge base.

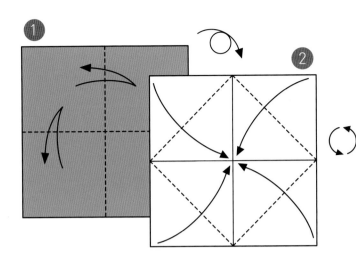

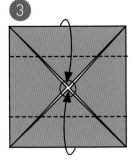

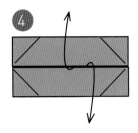

Bring it into the
center keeping
the flaps nicely still.

Lift it by opening
the inside flaps
together.

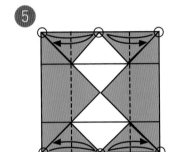

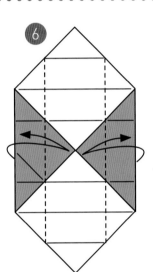

Mark the folds then
open the upper and
lower flaps.

Lift the sides to create two
crimps. We're moving into 3D.

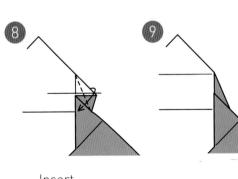

Insert.

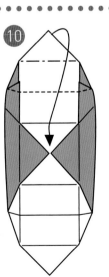

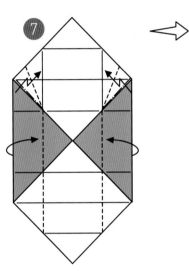

Repeat the
steps carried
out in diagrams
7, 8, 9 and 10
on the lower
side.

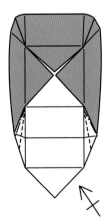

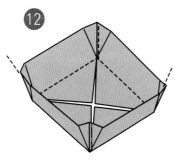

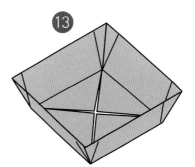

Taking the edges between two
fingers, shape the container
into a regular square.

....
....

JOINING THE MODULES TOGETHER

WEDGE BASE
See the *masu* box.

Use a sheet of paper the same size as the one
you used for the bowl, cutting it in half.

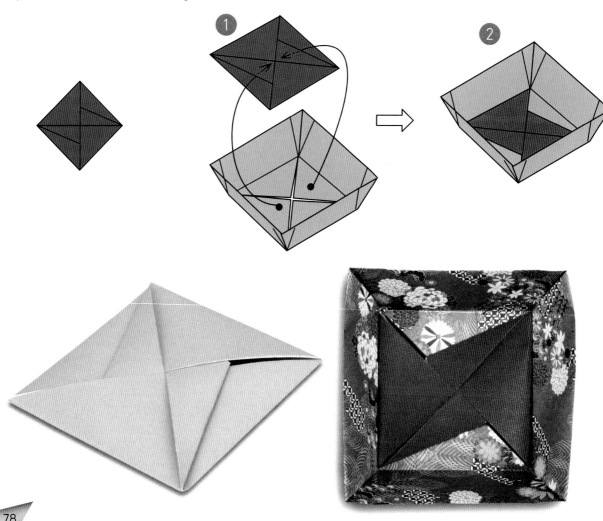

Paper:
standard
15 x 15 cm
(6 inches x 6 inches)

Cube box
with strip or wedge closing

This model requires many folds, which may make it appear difficult
to complete at first glance, but if you follow the fold lines shown exactly, the box will
take shape as if by magic. By giving it a reinforced base, you can use it as a gift box.

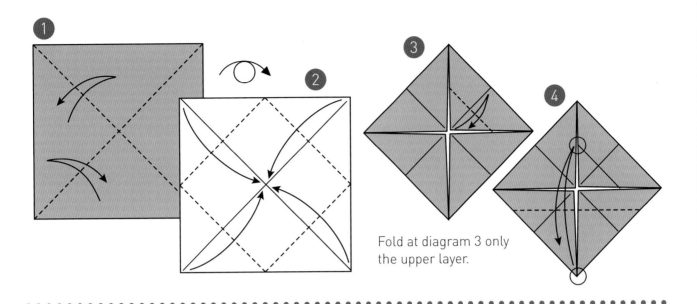

Fold at diagram 3 only
the upper layer.

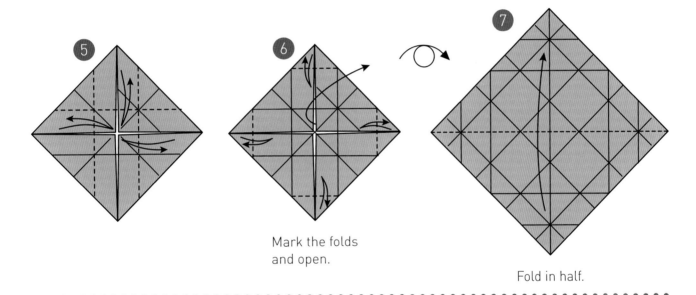

Mark the folds
and open.

Fold in half.

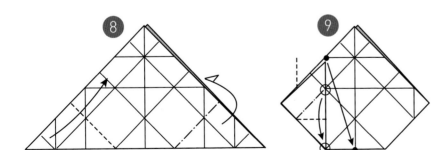

Repeat the steps carried out
in diagram 9 on the opposite
side, then open fully.

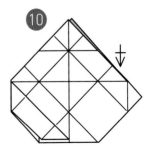

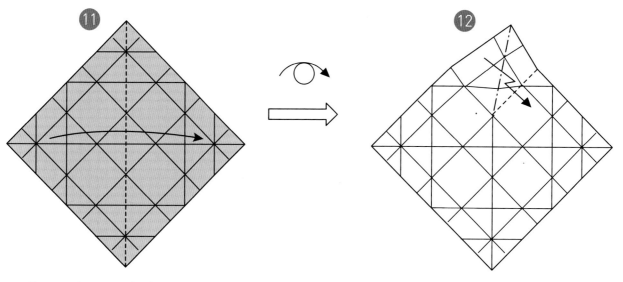

Repeat the steps in the diagrams
from 8 to 10, also folding along
the other diagonal, then open
fully.

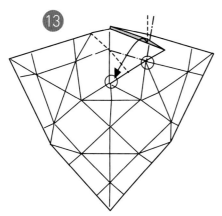

- Fold along the fold lines
marked in diagram 9.

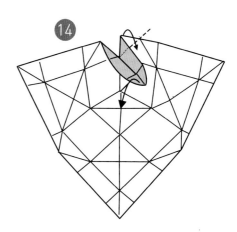

Intermediate steps.

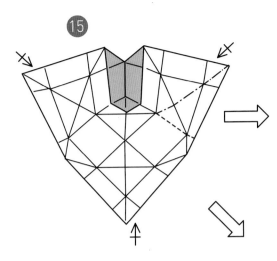

⑮

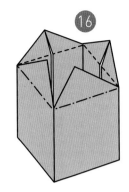

⑯

Mark the folds on the inside of the box.

Carry out the same steps at the other three points shown.

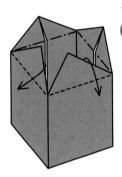

⑰

Fold and unfold the upper flaps.

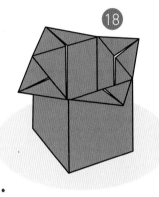

⑱

Your useful container is complete.

STRIP CLOSING

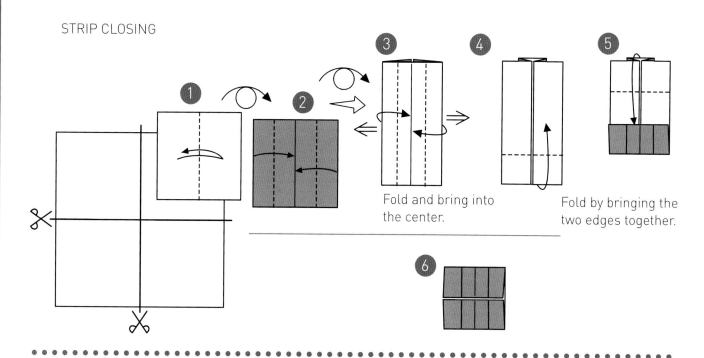

Fold and bring into the center.

Fold by bringing the two edges together.

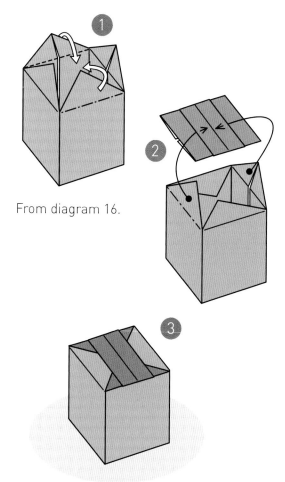

From diagram 16.

CUBE BOX WITH STRIP CLOSING

WEDGE CLOSING

Make the "wedge" as explained in the *masu* box but use a smaller rectangle as shown in this diagram.

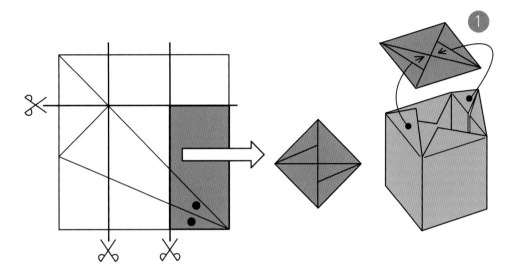

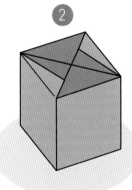

CUBE BOX WITH
WEDGE CLOSING

Paper:
20 x 20 cm
(8 inches x 8 inches)
or bigger

Double cube box

Adding further folds to the cube box makes an unusually shaped container reminiscent of two cubes merged together. The bigger the sheet of paper you use the easier it will be to make.

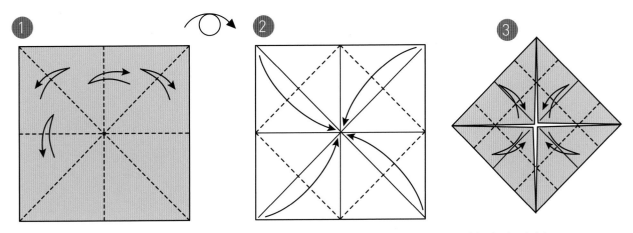

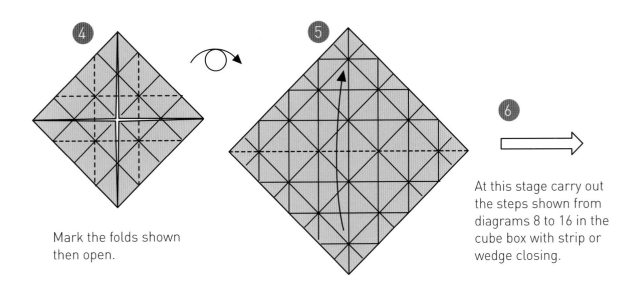

Mark the folds as
shown in the diagram.

Mark the folds shown
then open.

At this stage carry out
the steps shown from
diagrams 8 to 16 in the
cube box with strip or
wedge closing.

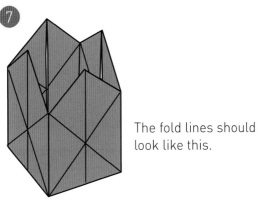

The fold lines should
look like this.

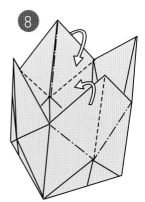

8 Fold both the front and back flaps towards the inside.

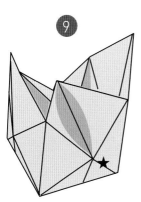

9 Intermediate step.

In the next diagram turn the model around as shown by the movement of the ★ symbol.

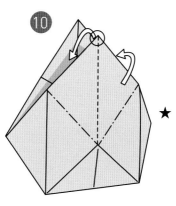

10 Fold the front flap towards the inside by pushing it in firmly so that the tip with the ○ symbol corresponds to the ◎ symbol in the next diagram.

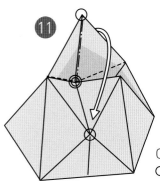

11 Overlap by bringing the ○ symbols together.

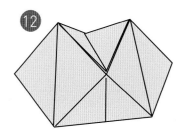

12 The model with two overlapping flaps.

(You may wish to consider the box finished at this point).

THE MODEL SEEN FROM THE BASE

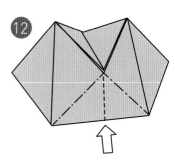

12 Make a hollow by pressing at the point shown by the arrow.

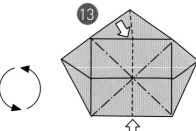

13

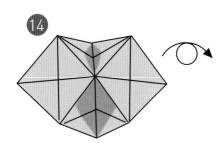

14

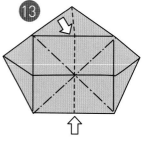

15 Fasten with an elastic band in the position shown in the diagram.

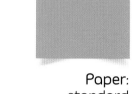

Paper:
standard
15 x 15 cm
(6 inches x 6 inches)

Tortoiseshell bowl

Making this hexagonal bowl with an inner support will improve
its solidity and appearance.

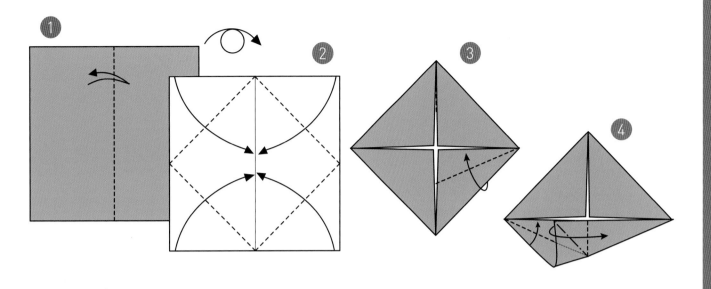

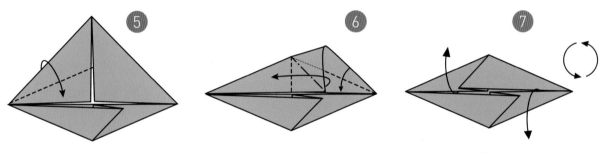

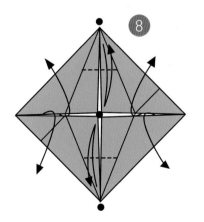

After marking the folds
unfold as in diagram 3.

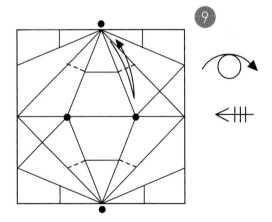

Fold by bringing the ● symbols together,
then open fully.

Fold by bringing the ● symbols
together.

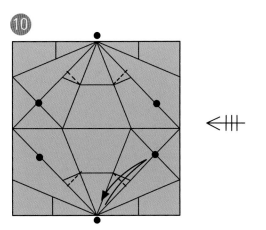

Fold by bringing the ● symbols together.

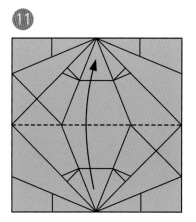

Fold in half.

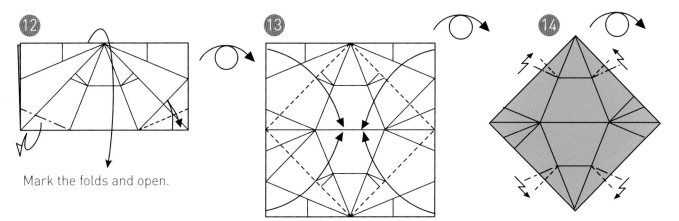

Mark the folds and open.

Mark the folds in the upper and lower layer then open fully.

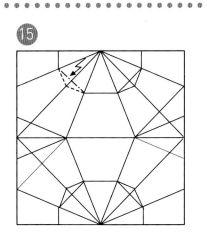

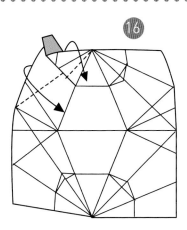

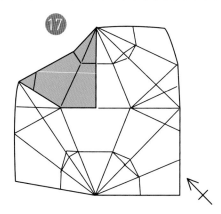

Repeat the steps carried out in diagrams 15 and 16 on the opposite side.

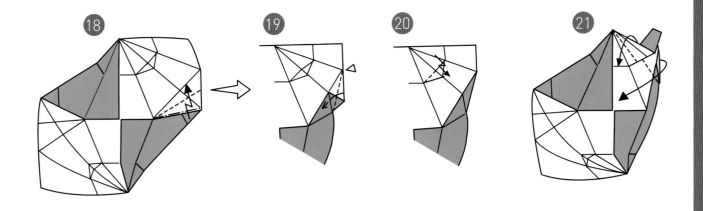

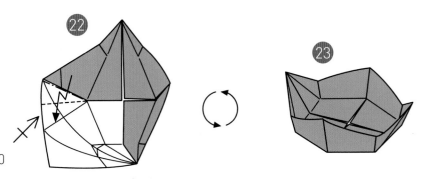

Repeat the steps carried
out in diagrams 19 and 20
on the opposite side.

DIAMOND BASE

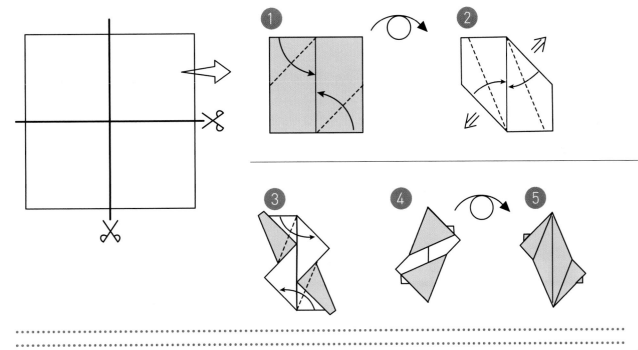

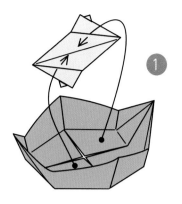

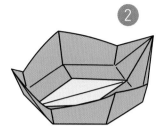

Base of bowl seen
from the inside.

Insert into the openings.

Paper:
standard
15 x 15 cm
(6 inches x 6 inches)

Tulip cup

The many folds required may make this model appear difficult, but remember that every step is repeated four times so proceed carefully, checking that each fold is correct before moving on.

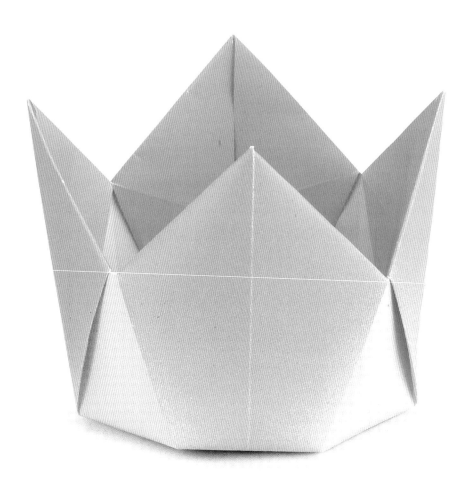

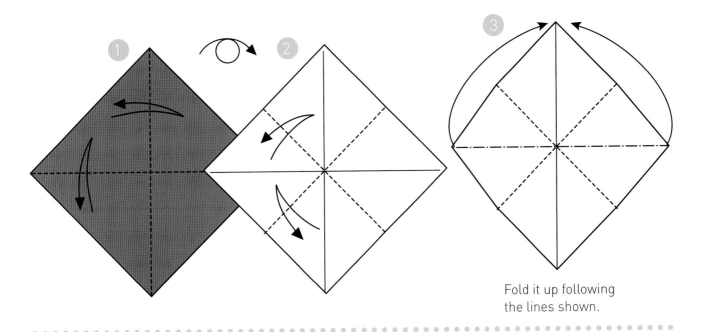

Fold it up following
the lines shown.

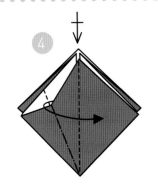

Carry out the same step
on the opposite side.

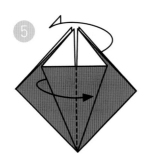

Make a book
fold.

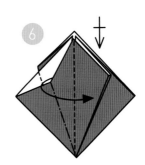

Open fully.

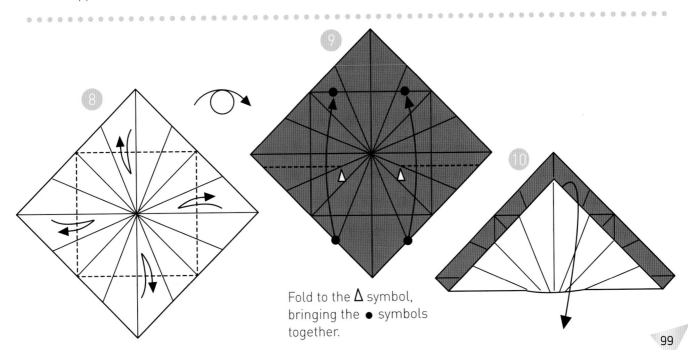

Fold to the **Δ** symbol,
bringing the ● symbols
together.

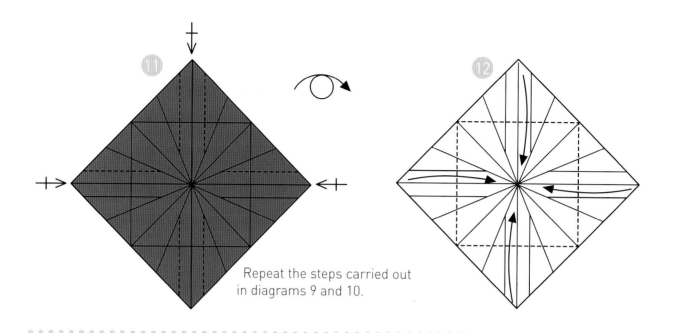

Repeat the steps carried out
in diagrams 9 and 10.

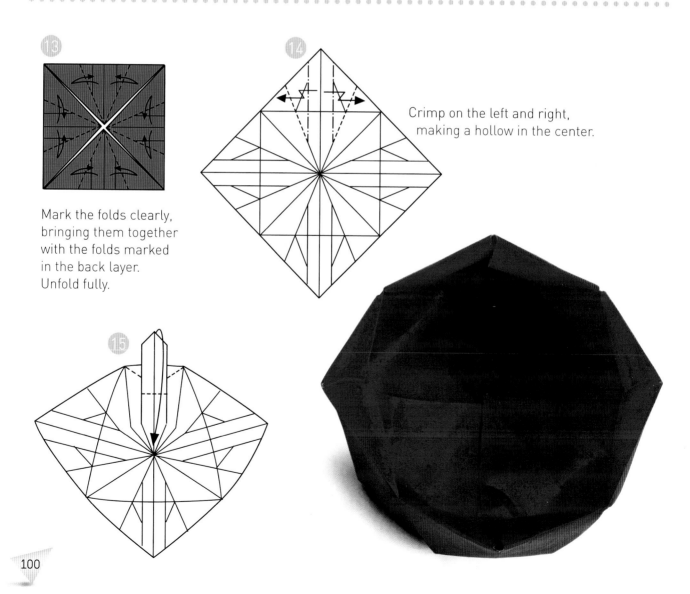

Mark the folds clearly,
bringing them together
with the folds marked
in the back layer.
Unfold fully.

Crimp on the left and right,
making a hollow in the center.

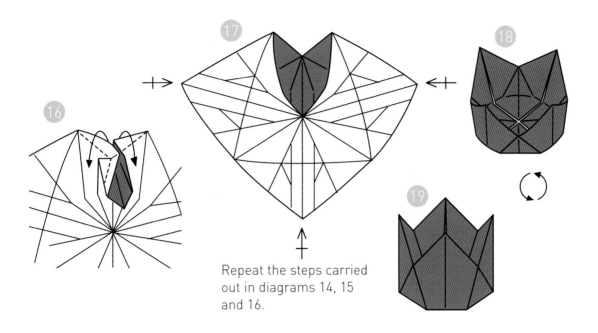

Repeat the steps carried out in diagrams 14, 15 and 16.

Paper:
standard
15 x 15 cm
(6 inches x 6 inches)

Flower box for sweets

A box for sweets embellished with a ring of eight petals.
Make it even more beautiful with an extra base.

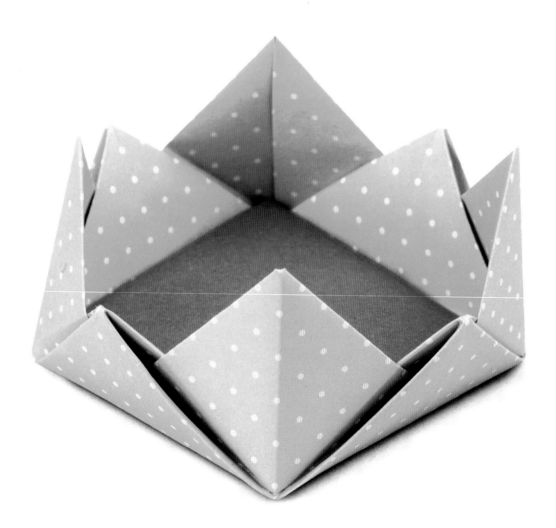

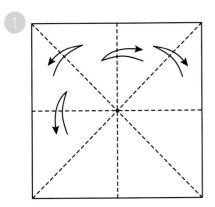

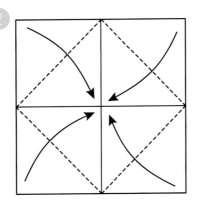

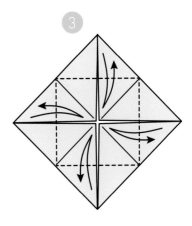

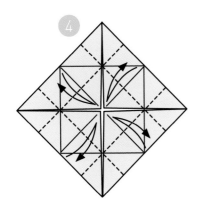

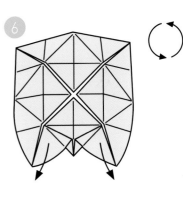

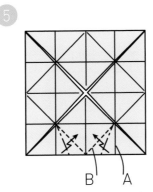

Trace both the folds then fold by bringing line A together with line B.

Unfold only the folds carried out in diagram 5.

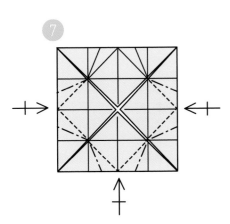

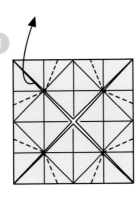

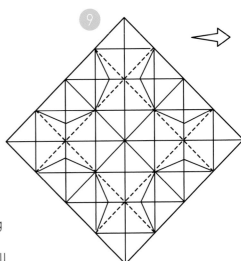

Repeat the same step at the other three points shown.

Make a valley fold along the lines marked as mountain folds. This will make it easier to close. After marking the folds unfold fully.

B   A

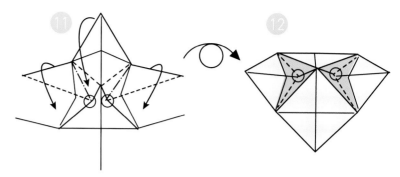

10 Bring these together making a hollow.

11 Intermediate steps.

12 The model seen from the colored side. Make a hollow at the points corresponding to the O symbols.

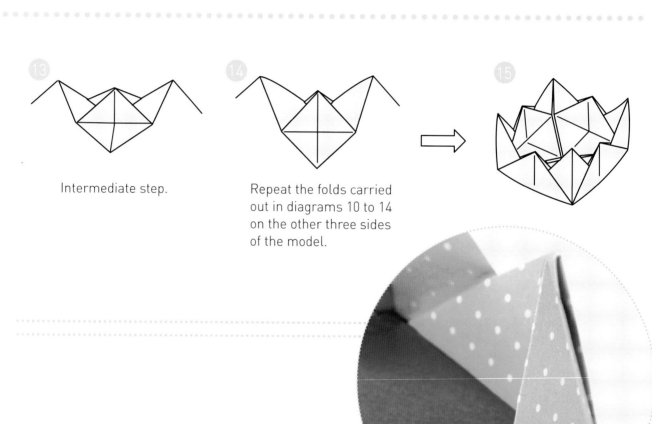

13 Intermediate step.

14 Repeat the folds carried out in diagrams 10 to 14 on the other three sides of the model.

15

WEDGE BASE

See the base of the *masu* box.

Use a sheet of paper the same size as the one you used for the box, cutting it in half.

1

Then insert the base turned upside down.

2

1

2

Base, inside part.

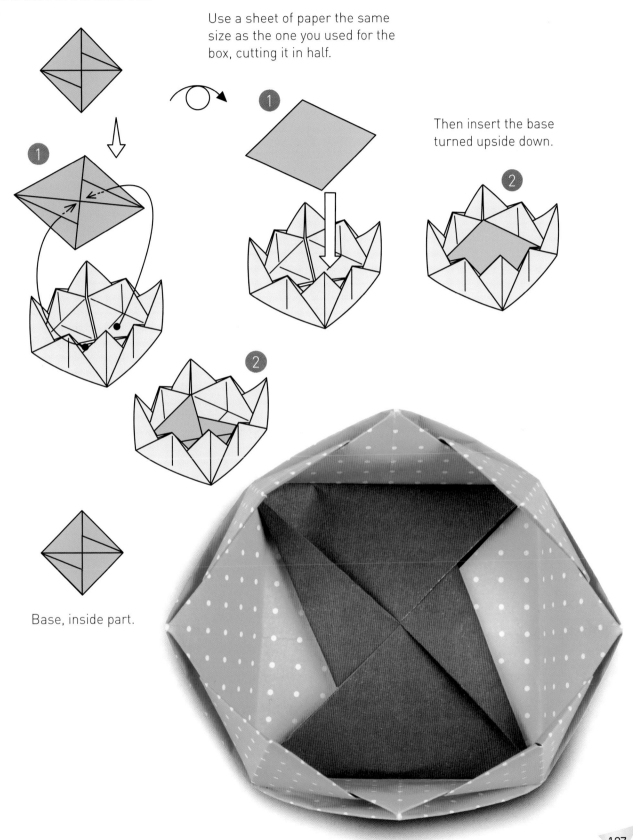

SQUARE BASE

Desired width.

1 Fold by bringing it towards the central line. It does not need to meet exactly.

2 Fold by bringing it to the edge.

3 Height of your choosing.

Fold by bringing it towards the central line. It does not need to meet exactly.

4 Fold by bringing it to the edge.

5 The arrows show the positions of the two pockets.

6

This base can also be used for other boxes. The dimensions can be varied as required.

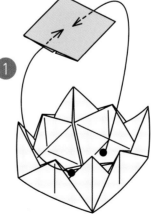

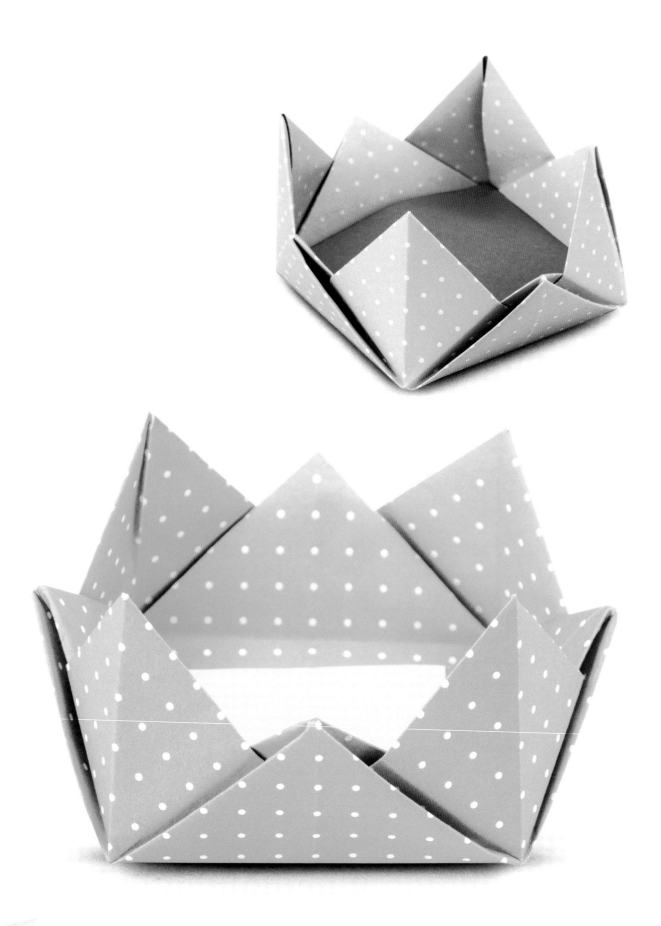

Paper:
standard
15 x 15 cm
(6 inches x 6 inches)

Rose box

You can make a single box and use it on its own, but by creating a variety
of different sizes and putting one inside the other your rose will be even more lifelike.

Mark the folds as shown in the first four diagrams.

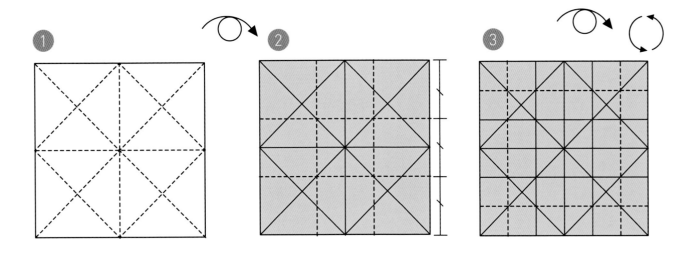

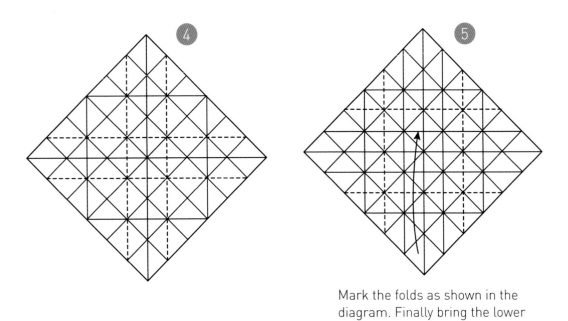

Mark the folds as shown in the diagram. Finally bring the lower flap towards the top.

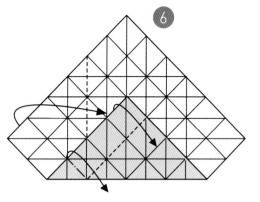

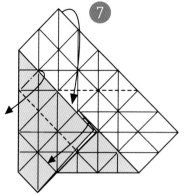

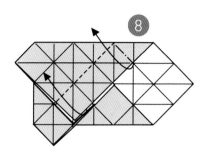

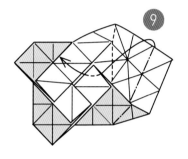

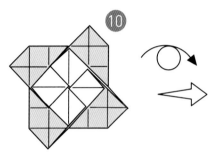

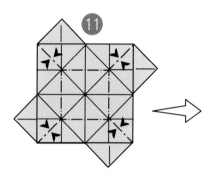

Give the model volume by holding the points corresponding to the ⌐ symbols with two fingers, creating a cube shape.

Twist by making a hollow in the center.

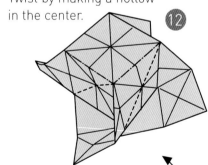

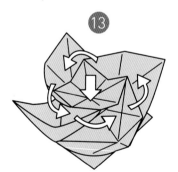

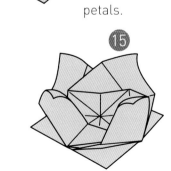

While collapsing it, press from above to flatten the base. This will cause the petals to lift.

Round off the petals.

The model seen from the other side.

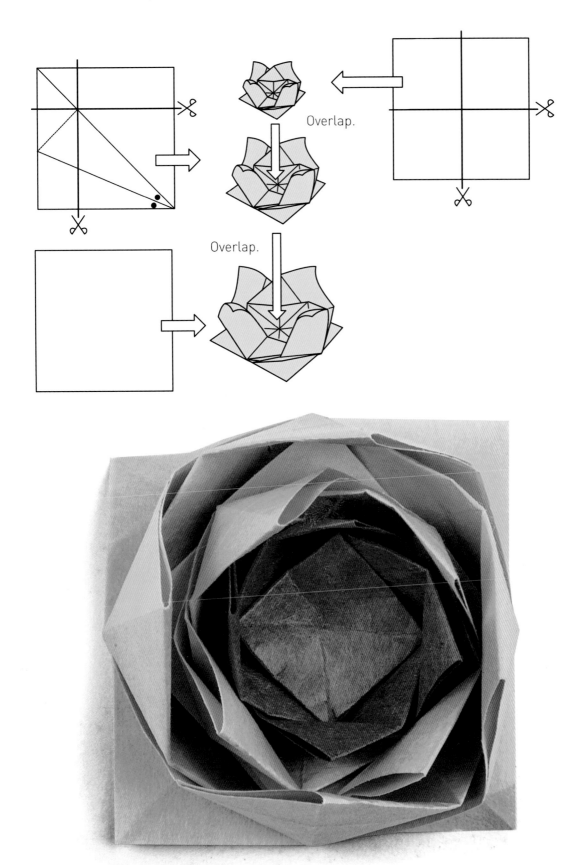

Overlap.

Overlap.

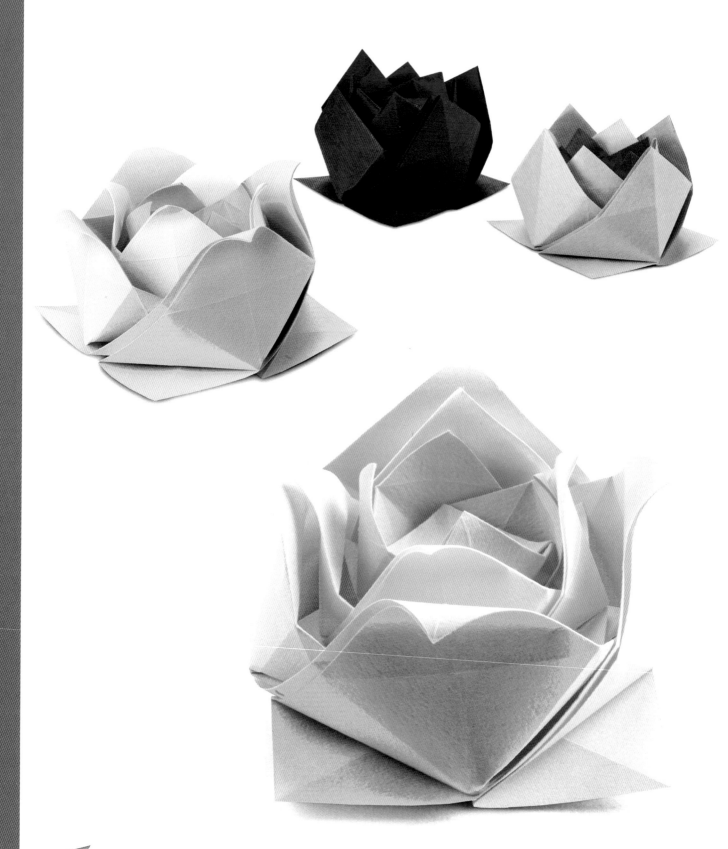